Seeing From
A Distance

Also by Catherine Anthony (Kitty Anthony)

The King's Castles

Seeing From
A Distance

Catherine Anthony

To order additional copies of this book, contact:
Xlibris Corporation
1-888-795-4274
www.Xlibris.com
Orders@Xlibris.com
35954

Contents

The eye never has enough of seeing,
  nor the ear its fill of hearing.
What has been will be again,
  what has been done will be done again;
there is nothing new under the sun.

Ecclesiastes 1:8, 9

The Circle

Eternity circles, trailing colors
pulsing with time's beat,
rising in ecstatic heat,
and cooling through creation's rounded
glory where it rides complete.

But there is dark that weaves and pricks
through matter terrified, obtuse,
while all about, like watching birds
above a drying, lifeless thing,
a hovering, fierce competitor
tries waiting out the Rescuer,

who will not be denied or end.
He knows each atom thrown in intimate
complexity, arranged and verified,
rarified as good, then needing
ultimate redemption so that
blood-drenched, pure and graced,
loved ones live unbroken, breathing glory.

2003

The View

I live in a jar that curving clarifies
and lights my soul's unbroken truth,
binds my breathing heart in comfort
because knowing is serene.

I view the world three-sixty, missing
no idea that matters now
or now, because I live in grace
without illusion that I valued
once what I could not keep.

2004

Today

The world is fragmenting, picked apart
by goodwill hunters, fevered by a
lonely Saturday night and dieting
at the beach while boys camouflaged
take a stand on eastern deserts,
holding off masked rivals like heroes.
And the philosopher drives a cab
asking who is responsible here
so we can induct him into the Hall of Fame.

Yet one more image on the screen
of narrow children leaning lightly
on their milkless mothers where
they sit with nothing living.
So the world offers up
another dish and gives a dollar
with a wish that we can do better.

Who can put the pieces back together?
and do we have enough to pay the bill
for all the strangled lives, their pockets
picked, left dying on damp
streets far from Eden.
How many miles to the gallon
must we buy to get there?
Will no one volunteer to bind
the wounds and stop the world from bleeding
out? If only one could save us.

continued

We would make him king.
Perhaps the One who made it
whole in the beginning
knows how the pieces fit.
Perhaps He has enough blood
to wash it white. I would not
be surprised if this were so.

2005

Luke Eleven

One tenth of rue, rosemary, mint
are but one tenth of all the leaves
that spring and flutter year by year,
woe by woe, herb harvest
trailing bitter scent that strangles
unredeemed for want of love.

2004

Prayer

Risen Lord, your child asks
one favor, one you granted once
when there before your unscarred feet
she knelt, not pleading any cause,
but loving Thee beyond herself.

Please Lord, that I may wash
with tears your resurrected feet
and dry them with my hair.

2002

What If?

What if no wind could move a forest tree?
The forest litters fallen trees—what is.
What if no mother left before her chick to die?
But mothers and their chicks must say goodby.
What if each wound could disappear without
a bloody tear? But wounds rain down rain down,
the reason for our fear—what is.

2005

Superman Crucified

"God? What God?" spoke Nietzsche, fallen
Superman shackled with the bonds
of his mind gone round the bend
of his own making, twisted
by his helpless hands into a knot
he could not break because alone.

"The first decent human being."
no one good enough to help him.
Dionysius splayed upon a cross
with no one there to see or care,
not even those who ran from him
to find their living elsewhere.

Along a narrow lane he searched for truth
and stumbled past it in his dark, blind
to the Sightgiver lifted high
for even Nietzsche who finally knows
unqualified truth.

2002

Oh my Chevalier

Chevalier, oh my, my Rescue
moves, rears to flight unopposed
striding riding sparking flinty
hooves beneath Him in the rocky
way to evermore. Oh
I ride with Him wearing robes
woven for only sons.

Angry teeth wait to swallow
wounded parts, devour leaking
soul, tripping-licking-sucking.
But the holy Champion roars,
stops the mouths, sweeping down
to darkness dark shapes whose
withered knight has lost his spurs.

2005

Meditation at 37,000 Feet

This pause, this impasse
in a life that wandered once
from silliness to dire,
sweetness to desire.
Never knowing consequence
could be so all or nothing
is an unsettled thing.

It has the look of same
with only small promise,
just an end of some
timely blink where
on the circling edge
it waits expecting wonder.

2003

For Oxford's Latimer, Ridley and Cranmer

The dead live their belief throughout
inexplicable eternity.
Their burning severed bonds that
fixed them just to earth.

The burners thought their land, a speck
of moist, ungiving earth between
the larger bits afloat in rolling
seas, too small to hold some other
minds' audacious thought,
dear, but theirs for cost.

Their cross is worth a troubled tear,
wonder that a nation's darkened
church would choose to flame the three
who could not live to fear eternal
death, when they knew One who,
dying for their living, lives.

1986

God's Grace

Sometimes softly, or with groans
we are stripped and face unclothed
so hot the sun and cold the wind and cruel,
the scathing stare of God to see our sin
that reds the once pale ivory purity
of spirit, cheek and breast, and arm
that reached to pull His pricey fruit
yet one more airy space to face.

But grace, most sure,
determined and secure,
can cloth my naked beating breast
and dress my spirit, cheek and arm
in light that pierces dark,
can wrap the beauty of the Christ
about my waiting, grieving heart
and fill my empty ark.

1997

"It is I"

He came to me across the water walking
through waves that built, fell and hissed,
a great apocalyptic Beast
striding, Judah's Lion crowned.

His path through roaring waves was straight
like glass, relentless, smooth and still.
Above us, misted skies gloomed and threatened,
heaping watery walls where I clung,
waiting for an end to all.

Then floating over roar and time, a word—
"Courage." With that, the ocean whorled,
lifting, leaving me without defense,
until, convinced that Heaven's Lord
Had spoken, I was not afraid.

Consummation

In quiet cruciform he lay,
but wondered why and could not ask,
his arms flung wide, his thoughts not meant
for prayer, his heart routinely beating.
But then, when light was failing from
the altar just behind his eyes,
a hand in scarred perfection touched
his dark and gave him sight.

So could he rise to stand alone
before his King still seated high
in blinding glory there?
How could he go from that still place
to walk in ordinary grace?
And though he could not see, he knew,
his face turned down, his eyelids draped
against the lightening throne,
that earth's veiled reality
is fired with close glory.

2003

A Death

The grave opens with the sound
of a silent sea, and through
the door a flat black spreads wide
to take the vacant thing, dressed
for meeting with the Guest of Honor
and those who stand to watch have parted
company with one they loved
more or less completely.
"Grief is the price they paid for love."

Once they sighed together, free
in April's garden but were never
free, content to be each other's
company, but now one stands
like a quiet stone before
High Heaven's jeweled throne,
and hears the holy roar and feels
the Shepherd's arms, a cradle of
enduring care, and knows for once
no fear because the price for love
was paid with grief unknown.

2003

If I Were Old

If I were an old woman dying,
I would speak of sorrows too,
Mr. Park, of lost things rare
and simple, beautiful and dark,
of feelings lost, ignored to cruel
intensity, words hated
for their power, their impossible
grip on a heart's incomplete
beating, lacking even comfort.

But after all the heart's complaint,
One Hope rides the currented air
on rich wings that sweep and hover,
waiting with indestructible joy.

2004

Two Paths

I turned to the left in that yellow leaved wood,
and walked four steps down a darkening path,
then more slowly, for a lowering mist
had steeped beneath a tangle moldering,
never still, but constantly adjusted
by pale busy things, their mouths gulping
ruined life no longer pulsing.
Back I traced to where I had begun
turning right, half ran beneath its green
feathered branches met in careful
arching just enough to fringe the sun's
neutral gold. I wanted promises.
Both paths were traveled wide and worn.
I wanted a voice, a sign. I needed more.

2004

Abraham

Live in the past? Not me, said he
who looked at stars as children moving
in eternal rounds of restless music
like his life forever alien here.
He had the word from far beyond the stars,
the promise incandescent, guaranteed
of multiplying life, so he knew
he could not live with disillusion now
or disappointment then, for he was
significant. His God was more.
And so he worshiped on his face.

2005

Sarah

Sarah laughed, and laughed again,
not believing, unaccepting
that her God could open up
her ancient womb, sequestering
a necessary patriarch
born to walk with his Creator.

Her husband should have known, for he
would make all of a nation, wide
as the earth spread deep with sandy
grains, each one an Abrahamic seed.
He rushed to offer hospitality
to Heaven's visitors and heard
the Living Word. "Next year
this time your wife will birth a son."

The angels waiting in the shade
of nearby trees had heard her laugh
and pressed their case, for after all,
the Lord who spoke all life in time
could surely will a child to breath
within old Sarah long past bearing.
But then her laughter terrified her,
so she lied to God.

And as her baby swelled to strength,
her husband watched her beauty
grow to dazzle, and waited for
the evidence of covenant.

2004

The Nail

The enemy, tucked up in camp was sleeping
hard between his spear and shield that slumped
against red carpet walls, his name, Sisera.

His army lay in blood beside a brook
of iron wheels that in the battle rushed
nine hundred thick toward their scheduled death.

Only this one stood, then ran, leaving
chariot and field to refuge in
a kinder place, with no one to command.

The tent he found was home to one who offered
milk and comfort, promises to watch,
and "Do not be afraid." Her name was Jael.

She knew his twenty years of thorny rule
until a nation cried like children to their
Lord, who answered when they knew

they could no longer live without Him,
"I will give him up, but not to Israel.
A woman shall take spear and shield and blood."

continued

Soft she stood and watched his sleeping face
above the covering she spread to warm him
where he lay, and knew that she would kill.

The woman watched his pulse beat above
his ear beside his tangled hair, then reached
to free a stake from underneath a pile

of pegs that might have held a tent in place.
She counted ten then twenty pulsing beats
then lifted from its box a battered tool.

She placed the pointy peg precise
and delicate above the beating skin,
his eye tight closed in dreamless sleep.

One second more, she waited, lifted arm
above her head, fingers tightened round
the woody handled tool for hammering.

Down she rammed the heavy thing until
the stake was lost within a bloody place,
and Jael was kneeling low before her God.

2003

Jonah

Rocked to fear on dark waves
of glassy weed that reached to knot
my arms and legs, my hair wound
fast, bound, torn, I waited,
knowing death, mourning life,
for I had fled from God,
my name a curse, a sneer, unfit
to bless or baptize children.

The fish had gulped me deep below
where, bathed in acid pools, I fainted,
hoping not to wake or think,
like one more fin or tail.
How could I cry to God? How?
I was no Lazarus listening for
a holy shout to open up the beast
for me to stride through toothy bars
and find friends waiting, weeping.
I had defied Jehovah.

Three days later I was standing
in sweet air, breathing holy words
because the King of Heaven reached
His glorious arm deep inside
the fish, took me by the neck,
wrenched me free and flung me
to an anxious, waiting world,
opened wide my mouth with love
and waited for my worship.

2004

Daniel

Deep inside the rocky earth and dark,
the teeth of beasts closed tight by holy hands
waited salivating for the promised feast,
he stood with wary eyes, watching, turning,
    longing
for his end but knowing that his Master
would do what He would do although he wept,
    reminding
Adonai of his obedience and love.

Hours passed until he sank on weakened knees,
and lay cold upon the stoney floor, while
lion-maned cats curled tightly at his feet.

First light, King Darius hurried to the den
to see a bloodied death, but he called in anguish
down through dark quiet. And standing ready
    for his
king to see his innocence, the man of God
waited to be lifted up and out to face
a hungry people who were unaware
the Son Himself can close the teeth of fear
and raise His child up from dark to light.

2005

Zechariah's Robe

He stood before God's mirror horrified,
unable or unwilling maybe both
to see his torn and spotted robe,
from neck to hem, behind, in front,
each mark grotesqued by careless sins
silted, layered, sickened raw.

Seeing all, he thought to tear away
his ruined robe and hoped to find beneath
some beauty, or at least a reason he could
give to argue, prove, substantiate
that he was clean, acceptable.

And then within the glass a face whose eyes
saw all, the measure of his soul unclothed,
underneath his wretched robe and all,
and foiled light reflected grace so that
his robe was torn from top to hem, exchanged
for fabric woven and reserved for sons.

2003

Christmas
(From St. John of Damascus)

The holy Lord, who cannot be contained,
no, not within the rolling universe that,
ringed with golden suns and sailing stars
is limited by boundaries somewhere,
entered one woman's womb, choosing
to sequester there until the time
of her deliverance, arranged before
one crystal sprang from Heaven's mouth
to shine in its appointed place in space.

Then He who planted Eden, where who knows,
and rained sweet manna from high Heaven, even
quail, and later broke five loaves in pieces
five thousand worth accompanied by two
fish, sustaining all creation since,
even wine that from sweet water sprang
for feasting with the Lamb, Himself drank
His mother's milk while folded in her arms
one soft night in Bethlehem's retreat.

His mother lifted to her heart her son
with loving hands, not knowing she held God
whom many winged seraphim transport,
trailing glory to His throne somewhere.
But she in love held Him on her knees.

2003

Easter 2004

Did Lazarus thank his Lord that day
when lying in his first pain-free
sleep, or seeing Paradise,
he heard the King who loved him shout
"Come out!" and stood on unsure feet
to walk, trailing draperies
of death from unlight out to see
the Light standing where He wept
for love of him whose flesh journeyed
full circle, no longer reeked
of worm or time, but scented resurrection.

Perhaps he sighed to see his sisters
wringing helpless hands, keening grief,
but then amazed that all their careful
cleansing, wrapping had not kept him
safe within, for he knew they
would have to do it all again,
and he would lose his breath and feel
his blood slow, his body wrenched
from breath to death one more time.

continued

He had obeyed his Christ, his friend,
and knew one joy the mourners could not
see, nor would until they walked
behind the veil to find their Loved One
in His majesty, His startling
robes declaring on His breast
the names of resurrected ones
who wear the draperies of life.

2004

Peter

Two ancient heros stood in close
with Him who knew them from the start,
while Peter and the others watched.
"Let's build for them three tents," he said,
that foolish man of rock, "and live here
on this mountain peak,"
whose eyes like fire, His face and hair
like sun on new snow.

Poor silly man who thought that he
must live on mountains so his earthbound
cousins could not cast him down
to perish in their busy seas or worse.
It's not enough to talk the ancient
prophet talk while millions wounded
walk all day toward eternal night.

So down he came to fish for men
and eat beside his God until
some bully spread him wide upon
a rough inverted cross, the better
to look up and see his Christ
whose ready arms would press him
to His glittering breast.

2005

Prodigality

He sat among the pigs, hunched
over empty hands, bent,
ragged, weeping for his life,
lost by his own device,
shoeless, narrow, empty, want-
ing all, having none.

(One day he took, then ran with half
his father's treasure far as it
could take him, spent his busy play
that nailed his soul to stone, where
dying, lying at the bottom
of the earth, he wondered what if.)

"I know who you are," claimed
Unknown. Then growing light
bloomed widely, and he knew
that he would live again if only
as a slave or worse. He heard,
he stood, he moved to find his home.

He did not know his father would not
leave off looking for the child
he loved, because he would not turn
from the one who had abandoned him,
but give him treasured grace instead.

2006

Easter 1999

Tell me, Lord,
Do you still feel each thorny point
around your priceless crown?
And does the memory live
of knotted blows that savaged flesh
once mother-kissed, caressed beside
a manger in King David's town?

Or does each hammered stroke still tear
your loving hands that touched unblinded eyes,
capped the silky heads of babes and
palmed the swirling universe with light?

And can it be you feel the woody plank
along your ravaged spine, your muscles torn
and wrenched from ligaments to bone?
But worse, is all that Father love
remembered lost for one dark day,
as if He turned His back and left you
there once more the target of
a thoughtless, thankless world?

All this because of me, for me.
Dear Christ, this day I pray, that you
remember only Resurrection,
that we remember Resurrection.

1999

Going to Emmaus

The two of us walked and mourned,
all our hopes in fragments,
pieces that we could not reassemble.
So when another joined us on the road
we told him all our sorrows, wept
because our disappointment was
so large it choked our faith, our hope.

Our Lord had come and gone without
considering our loss it seemed,
for we had been abandoned.
Where were we to find another king?
"What did you expect?" the listener said.
"Your prophets told you He would live
and die, this way, this truth, this life."

His words accused us in their comfort,
lighting firey passions
in our fading spirits as we talked.
He would have gone away, it seemed,
when wanting not to break the thread
between us, we invited him
to sit with us, to share a meal.

continued

Then he held the bread, praying
breaking pieces with familiar hands,
now scarred, while we looked
beyond our sorrow, seeing
only Him, knowing Him.
What king abandons sons redeemed
with blood and love? Not my king.

2005

Good Grief

A grief comes round to meet me
where I am with no one near
to help me understand the sorrow
I had made, a lively death
kept in circling discontent.

But then the circle turned me round
to see another grief, reflected
and exposed and springing from
the center, starred by Holy heat
that made me shield my eyes and look
within where, once my eyes adjusted
to the shining, I found waiting,
knowing all, One who drove me
to His side, rich with grace.

There I was at home, returned
to unhurried rest, though
stricken by my guilt. I wept,
grieved because His bloody death
was all my fault. He offered joy,
for He had meant it all for love.

2003

The Rescue

I wrestled in a grip complete
Of spiney fingers nailed with death
And dipped in carrion lives long gone.
No matter where I turned or groaned
Or pled for mercy, bled for time,
The gripping was unmoved but tighter,
Set to ripping, tearing each bloody
Drop away that fed my living.

But round the circle of my soul,
Three words—a holy voice engraved
Them there—"She's mine." With that,
I reached to touch God's face
And all else fell away.

2004

Treasured Terror

Help me walk on water, Lord.
The ground beneath my feet is no less
insecure than rising waves,
twisted tides and chilling spray
that drives me to my knees to pray,
to grope for holy hands to lift me
high above this world's dark,
cold threatening roar and hiss.

Across the boiling world, one voice
comes singing notes that play and dance,
to meet me where my terrified
and sinking heart have forced me
to my face to lie subjected
there to wait for rescue.
"Take my hand," He said.

That shining day of undespised joy,
touched lightly through by holy fingers
sifting soul and blood, marrow,
numbered hairs and all, I leaned
against the holy Shepherd's breast.

I should have been afraid and was,
that cradled in His glory there, I could
have withered in close proximity
to perfect power; but I was robed,
wrapped in stuff blood-lined, delightful.

2003

Comfort

My knees, my heart are bent
before the face of Holy
who waits to offer more
than I know I want,
although my sweat in bloody
drops falls into the lap
of God where I have laid
my head at last in refuge.

2003

Knowing Comfort

Knowledge is sorrow and truth will free
the wanderer to weep and gasp
for breath in spite of comforters who
uninvited dare the fallen one to trust
and worse, appear in threes or fours.

Such knowledge must be borne, must light
and crack the stone-walled chambers where
some rich upholstered comfort waits
and withers in the glare of positive,
of document, of certain sure.

Such sorrow unrelieved is met
each time the circle turns, delivers
blow and blow that threatens air
from rushing heart to crown and down,
but still it must be born until
Sorrow's Man invites, "Don't cry."

2003

Please

Bright Lord of Heaven, time, space
pray, turn your eyes away, please do,
nor look at my frail soul, my flawed
and restless life, despaired.

Lord, shine no holy glare to light
my twisted, fragile frame in air,
exposed like moon and stars for all,
for even Heaven's seraphim
to know my wounded self, self-wounded.

Do not leave me there, my Lord.

2003

Worship

God of creation, heaven, earth, man
Whose name too high to think or speak,
Whose glory more than I can know,
Or would, until I stand before
Your throne, so glorious and high,
I cannot, dare not look, but bow
And listen to your voice and know
Thy pure consuming love for me.

Accept me as your own adoring child,
And keep my broken heart within your own,
Forever clean with blood that poured from
Gracefull wounds, oh Christ my Lord, my own.

1994

Song

God's glory pierces earthly dark,
His children see its shining,
Lay their willful minds before Him,
Face His fierce love and adore Him.

We bow, Oh Christ, before thy cross,
Deny our hearts to serve Thee,
Burn our indifference to Thy throne,
Fire our passion for You alone.

Holy Spirit living in us,
Comfort, strengthen, guide, inspire,
Touch our lives with holy zeal,
To serve Thee and thy love reveal.

1986

Father

Enough of sparrows falling and
of sheep whose names you call!
They cannot know a daughter's pain
who leaves her fragile father
fallen in a heap and lying,
head turned so his tears seeped
through ancient creases in his face
because he cannot see her,
and he, the last of family there.
And she, the only one who cared
that he was.

Why, why, my Father,
must your cherished son
lie so piteously wounded?
"You're all I have," he said.
I've buried son and wife
in three years time."

Why? Why is sorrow
never far, a heartbeat near?
Is there a reason, Lord of all,
we live our days from pain to pain,
with now and then a sweet
moment of relief?

1994

Mothers Day

The day that I became full grown,
before my girlhood quite had flown,
I turned to find her waiting near,
tender, honest, loving, dear.
But rushing on to womanhood
I stopped impatient where she stood
to listen quickly, wanting less
than she would give to me, I guess.
"Remember, my daughter, chickadee,
whatever it is you want to be
you can. And never forget I love you."

Now I am a woman grown
and still she waits with love to hear
how I have lived and learned, or no,
I fear she's disappointed though.
But never does the day begin
that I don't love her more
than the day before.

Animal Stuffed
(After a visit to the nursing home)

A grinning beast with hair acrylic
stares through sightless beads a look
though hard I try, I cannot mimic.
And even though I grin and smirk
the chubby bear returns no hint
of reciprocal acknowledgment.
It keeps no confidence I share
nor hears my teary plight.

But once I walked down halls at night
to find one old and shrunken thin,
a body sucked to boney wrinkles,
woman once, but now a thing.
She slumped inside a plastic chair,
her arms hung loose around a bear,
a fuzzy, solemn child's thing
imprisoned with its partner, dying,
waiting for her turn to leave.
No one comes to see them there.

1998

A Woman by Any Other Zoo Would . . .
(After "A Woman at the Washington Zoo")

That buzzard pecking up the grain
in rushing jabs beside a lioness is bold
and just a little foolish,
for the cat could sweep the fowl
between her pointed jaws,
a single move.

The woman there without the cage,
a neutral life, without, without,
who undesired, aimless there,
a caverned space within,
would wrap the bars of captivating
need around her nest if she could,
her freedom only then complete
in one man's hands.

1969

Baja

The quiet sea in silver ribbons
holds the far-off Coronados
in two gray, mysterious molds.
I'd like to stand so close that
I could touch each island,
and I might find the soul of dreams,
significant dreams.
For what are these except the
glittering sun upon reality,
but far enough away, the truth
seems more appealing than
at close touch.

Standing on the Baja beach
I held my shoes and pushed
with grainy toes the sand
in mounds and valleys, drawing
rounds in some unknown
unspoken language of the heart.
And knowing I would find no
great discovery there,
I left the moving shore to find
my private miracle elsewhere.

1968

Poem

The pure and new
begin as wise.
The end is rue,
entangled ties.
Those who stand
between are sure
there is no wisdom.

1968

Friend

Frailty cast a green memory
half hidden by grasses
shoulder high whose roots
are only wishes.

1969

One Truth

Possession is a myth
living in the dreams
of the uninitiated.
With the disillusion
in fearful clarity,
we own nothing
beyond the original gift.
Each one's significance
is sufficiency.

Each flower has its scent.
Each river has its source.
Each person has a soul.

What we might give
is not worth the giving.
What we try to give
is ruined, refused, or lost.

1968

The Joke

Rules for lovers, players and banks
are made by winners.
No abandon takes the game
but craft, device and speed.
This unrelieved maturing
men call life, and living,
play to win.

At last, the man, his treasures spread,
a final cold accounting,
recalls the cost, and then begins
the laughing, grim and old,
and wrinkled like his hands,
a laugh that threatens, shakes, erupts
in coughing, gray despair,
volcanoed by death-rattling truth.

No monster joke for such an end,
but yet a sixty-five year joke
we play on one another,
this living just a shivaree.
One instant more, the lesson lies
a coffined secret known to only
One who Heavenly seated, laughs.

1967

Vanity

It is vain to eat the bread of sorrows,
to smack the lips and suffer,
indulgent self, following
the coffin to the grave, to mourn
to weep for losing a holder, a prop,
a post, a tidy place for love.

And when the weight of breath
chest high, a lump that will not
dissipate, is fixed for one
who cannot keep appointments,
you wait for the thousandth time
since twenty or thirty or so.

1969

Joy

There is no happy, just a word.
Expectations melt with living,
one moment almost there
and straining to appear,
a show of wishes tinged with gold,
desired for their price, their claims
of glory laurelled in a minute's
song that fades and wisps away.

There is pure holy, word unspoken,
unexpected, growing joy
unrecognized at first until
it leaps from heart to knee and back,
unbidden but redeeming.